# Dinosaurs
# For Kids

# Amazing Animal Books
# for Young Readers

by John Davidson
Mendon Cottage Books

*JD-Biz Publishing*

**Read More Amazing Animal Books**

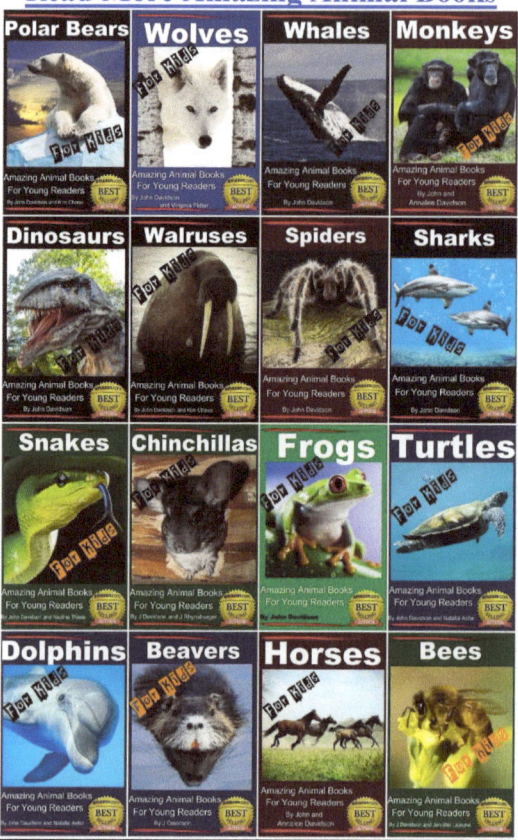

**Download Free Books!**
**http://MendonCottageBooks.com**

# Table of Contents

1. Introduction to Dinosaurs ........................................................ 4

2. Facts about Dinosaurs ........................................................... 7

3. Dinosaur Extinction ............................................................ 10

4. Dinosaur Fossils ............................................................... 12

5. Dinosaur Eggs ................................................................. 14

6. Dinosaur Names ............................................................... 15

6. Dinosaur Names ............................................................... 15

7. Dinosaur Diet ................................................................. 18

8. Feathered Dinosaurs ........................................................... 20

9. Plant Eating Dinosaurs ........................................................ 23

10. The Weirdest Dinosaurs ....................................................... 25

11. The Deadliest Dinosaurs ...................................................... 29

12. Flying Dinosaurs ............................................................. 32

13. Kinds of Dinosaurs ........................................................... 36

14. The Biggest Dinosaurs ........................................................ 39

15. The Smallest Dinosaurs ....................................................... 42

Publisher ....................................................................... 50

# 1. Introduction to Dinosaurs

The introduction of dinosaurs is with the Tyrannosaurus Rex dinosaurs. These are found in the world's biggest dig sites of Montana. Here paleontologists can explore the past of the dinosaurs existence and can know the secret of their life from the period of Cretaceous or Jurassic. The dinosaur can be huge, weird tiny and even wonderful. They are also termed as giant killers.

The word dinosaur is derived from the ancient Greek word which is denios. This means terrible lizard. They are a creature who are land dwelling and the dominated the life on this planet during Mesozoic Era which is 225 to 65 million of year ago. They were also flying reptiles along with being a marine reptile. The different types of marine reptiles are Plesiosaurs, Ichthyosaurs and Mosassaurs. They had their existence for nearly 150 million years. It occupied every kind of environment and climates on earth. They can see small as the size of chicken to over large ones being 100 feet long and having the weight of 100 tons. Dinosaurs evolved with time as the large structure and size has not been achieved overnight. The dinosaurs are two types the one called as Ornithischia which means bird hipped and Saurischia which means lizard hipped. The dinosaurs were herbivorous, carnivorous and also omnivorous.

*Tyrannosaurus Rex*

These are long extinct animals. Microraptor is a predator which was huge and had the ability to glide. They were even called marine reptile. The introduction of dinosaur can be done by classifying them as feathered or non-feathered variety. The dinosaurs are referred using their scientific name and also their genus and species. The dinosaurs are divided according to their geological period. The major groups in which these are divided are ovipators, sauropods, stegosaurs, dromeosaurs, ankylosaurs, ceratopsians and hardosaurs. The introduction of dinosaurs saw a very large variety along with different features of these animals. Different kind of them had different eating habits and place of their existence.

Microraptor
© Michael Rosskothen - Fotolia.com

# 2. Facts about Dinosaurs

Have you ever heard of Dinosaurs? What are they? Here are important facts about them.

1. Dinosaurs are reptiles that lived on earth over 230 million years ago.

2. The world Dinosaur originated from Greek meaning terrible lizard.

3. Dinosaurs are extinct and cannot be found on earth alive right now but their fossils can be extracted for study.

4. The heaviest dinosaur weighed about 80 tones, it was called brachiosaurus. Brachiosaurus had a height of 16 meters and a length of 26 meters. Its skeleton is kept in a museum on earth having the record of the greatest skeleton ever stored.

5. Dinosaur laid eggs which can be found in many shapes .The eggs can be 30 centimeters in length. The smallest egg of a dinosaur ever found on earth is about 3 centimeters in length.

6. When dinosaur eggs become fossils they harden like rocks but maintain their structure.

7. Troodon is the most intelligent dinosaur .It used to hunt, its length is

about 2 meters .Its brain was equal to the brain of the present day mammal .It had grasping hands and stereoscopic vision.

Fight between Euoplocephalus tutus and Troodon formosus

8. Ostrich mimic ornithomiminds was the fastest dinosaur .It was able to reach maximum speeds of 60 kilometers per hour.

9. The oldest dinosaurs which are 230 million years old were found in Madagascar.

10. Micropachycephalosaurus is the longest name of a dinosaur which means tiny thick headed lizard .It was discovered through fossils that were found in China.

11. Thecodontosaurus Antiquus was the oldest dinosaur to be discovered in Britain .It was discovered in 1970 in a place near Bristol. It was 2.1 meters in length and depended on vegetation for food.

12. Up to present over 700 species of dinosaurs have been discovered and named. Paleontologists are carrying out more research with an aim of discovering more.

13.108 species of dinosaurs have been discovered in Britain alone.

14. Megalosaurus was the first dinosaur to be formerly named. It was named in 1824.

# 3. Dinosaur Extinction

The term extinction is used in biology to refer to the end of an organism species or type. Dinosaurs became extinct 65 million years ago at the end of a time called the Creatureous period. Since this took place very many years ago, it is hard for scientists to find the reason that caused the dinosaur extinction. The rocks and fossils are used by the scientists to give clues on what happened are not so clear on what caused the dinosaur extinction. However, there are some probable reasons that have been put forward to try and explain what happened.

The reasons put forward include:

**Volcano eruptions**

Volcano eruption is on of the suggested reasons. According to this suggestion, there was a lot of volcanic activity that later caused changes in the weather. The dinosaurs were not able to adapt to the weather changes and so they died.

**Diseases**

Diseases could also have caused the death of the dinosaurs. The disease could have spread rapidly among them killing all of them.

## The Ice age

After some time, the earth becomes cold or cool. These periods are called ice ages and when they occurred the dinosaurs could have died from the cold as they cannot warm their bodies as we do.

## Asteroid impact

Scientists believe that a very big asteroid hit the earth destroying plants. This made the plant eating dinosaurs die of hunger. The meat eating ones then lacked food since the dinosaurs that they fed on had died and they died too.

## Combined reasons or Gradual extinction

It is also likely that some of the above reasons might have worked together to cause the dinosaurs extinction.
You should also remember that before the death of all the dinosaurs, there was a gradual decrease in their number. This might have been caused due to diseases and volcano eruptions all happening at the same time.

# 4. Dinosaur Fossils

Dinosaurs are earthly animals that existed some years ago. They are of different sizes and colors. Some have wings and other appear in their own physical appearance. Normally, the dinosaur fossils have been found to exist most in China. The main place where dinosaur can be found in China is called Shandong location.

This location is believed to have several dinosaur fossils with proof. Walking along this region in China will inform anyone that truly dinosaur lived there, prior time. Have you been asking people about where is the world's most dinosaur fossils found? From this content, it is proven that China Shandong region has the best response. Though, there are other places in China that also have dinosaur fossils deposit.

Another place in China that people can find dinosaur fossils is Zhucheng city. This place is popularly called the home of dinosaur. People that lived in this region prior, this time can tell more about the evolution of dinosaur. From this point, you can be sure to find dinosaur fossils in Zhucheng region of China. History and proof have made it clear that the world most center for dinosaur fossils is China.

You can have these places memorizing when you always want to talk about dinosaur fossils. Shandong and Zhucheng are the places that you can always think of when it comes to the case of dinosaur fossils. Many deposit of the dinosaur fossils can still be found there until today.

*Dinosaur Fossil*

They are kept in the zoo and gallery for people to see how they look like. The fossils are broken into parts for people to understand how the body of a dinosaur looks like. In case you have not see dinosaur fossils, it can be found in reading books for your interest. Remember that if you are looking for the largest place to find dinosaur fossils. You can always call Shandong and Zhucheng of China.

# 5. Dinosaur Eggs

Dinosaur's eggs have been found all over the world. Some of them are very similar to large ostrich eggs found today. They have been fossilized over time and that is why we can still find them today. They generally tend to be more symmetrical and rounder than bird eggs that we are used to today. Like the picture below the baby dinosaurs found in fossilized eggs can be studied to learn more about the nature of these wonderful animals.

Dinosaur Egg

# 6. Dinosaur Names

The following are common dinosaur names and their meanings. The dinosaur parts were discovered in fossils where the names were given according to the place of discovery or the part of an animal which the fossil resembled. Mostly they resembled lizards that is why they are given names relating to ordinary lizards.

1. Albertosaurus -Lizard of Alberta, was discovered in Alberta
2. Allosaurus -Strange Lizard due to its unusual bone
3. Apatosaurus-Deceptive Lizard
4. Baryonyx -Heavy Claw because the first fossil to be found was a claw
5. Brontosaurus Thunder Beast
6. Coelophysis -Hollow form
7. Cynognathus -Dog jawed ,has a jaw like that of a bird
8. Deinonychus -Terrible hand, because it looked like a hand during discovery
9. Dilophosaurus -Two-crested lizard
10. Dimetrodon -Two size of teeth
11. Dimorphodon Two types of teeth had close appearance to the teeth
12. Diplocaulus- Double stalk
13. Diplodocus -Double beamed lizard
14. Dolichorhynchops -Long-nosed snout
15. Dromaesaurus -Running lizard
16. Elasmosaurus -Thin plated lizard

17. Gallimimus -Bird mimic ,looks like a bird

18. Giganotosaurus-Giant lizard of south

19. Hesperonis- Regal western bird

20. Ichthyosaurus -Fish lizard

21. Iguanodon -Iguana tooth, the fossil resembled the tooth

22. Kronosaurus- Titan lizard

23. Liopleurodon -Smooth-sided teeth

24. Maiasaurus -Good mother lizard

25. Megalodon -Big-toothed shark. The fossil discovered resembled teeth of an ordinary shark

26. Mosasaurus- Meuse lizard, due to its resemblance

27. Nothosaurus - False lizard

28. Ornitholestes-Bird robber

29. Ornithomimus-Bird mimic, looks like an ordinary bird

30. Oviraptor- Egg thief, because they were believed to be taking eggs of other animals

31. Plesiosaurs -Close to lizard

32. Pliosaurs -More lizards

33. Protoceratops-First horn face

34. Pteradactyl- Winged lizard, believed to possess wings

35. Pteranodon -Winged, without teeth

36. Quetzacoatlus- Like Quetzalcoat

37. Saltopus -Jumping Foot, because the fossil that were first discovered resembled that of foot

38. Spinosaurus- Thorn lizard, because it resembled the thorn lizard

39. Stegosaurus- Roofed lizard because it had bones on the back

40. Suchomimus -Crocodile mimic because it looks like a crocodile in appearance

41. Triceratops -Three-horned face

42. Trilobites- Three lobes ,this is according to the resemblance of the body parts

43. Troodon- Wounding tooth

44. Tyrannosaurus Rex -Tyrant lizard

45. Utahraptor- Robber from Utah,this was named after the place it was first discovered

46. Velociraptor- Speedy robber

47. Yangchuanosaurus -Yanchuan Lizard

# 7. Dinosaur Diet

The dinosaur diet was mostly made up of plants and meat. Some dinosaurs ate plants. This is what is usually called a herbivore diet. Most of the dinosaurs were herbivores. These dinosaurs used their blunt teeth to chew the different plants. They ate leaves from trees, grass, and roots. Since dinosaurs were very big and tall animals, they ate a lot of plant matter to help them grow. Some of them stored food in their mouth for some days. To help the food digest, they swallowed rocks and sand. They also drunk a lot of water and always slept after eating.

Some dinosaurs were carnivores. The word carnivore means those dinosaurs that eat meat. These types of dinosaurs hunted down other animals for their meat. They were a threat to the dinosaurs that ate plants. The meat eaters could run very fast and catch the animal that they want to eat. They had big mouths with sharp teeth to help them remove the meat from the bones of dead animals. They were also very strong. Their strength helped them to hunt down animals that were sometimes bigger than they were. They also used this strength to fight with other animals that tried to steal their food.

Other dinosaurs ate both meat and plants. We call these kinds of dinosaurs as omnivores. Omnivores can eat any kind of plants and they hunted down other animals. These kinds of dinosaurs were very few. To get their food, they used to eat insects, birds, and they sometimes hunted bigger animals. Other times, they ate plants. They could eat the leaves growing on trees, grass, and any other kind of plants. These kinds of dinosaurs were very lucky as they can survive easily when there is no food. They were big and could move very fast when they are hunting for meat to eat.

# 8. Feathered Dinosaurs

The discovery of the partial pieces of skeleton by the Shandong Tianyu Museum suggests that some dinosaurs had feathers. A small skeleton of a dinosaur proved this theory right. The fossils found in the sediments also suggest of the existence of these feathered variety of dinosaurs.

China is famous for the fossils of its feathered dinosaurs. The fossil of the dinosaur that has been found in China is of the member of Heterodontosauride family, which is very primitive. These dinosaurs survived in the Cretaceous era and had very complex and distinguished teeth. The meaning of Heterodontosaurids is a lizard with different tooth, and they had advanced dentition. Their teeth were pointed, sharp and oversized and their back jaws were broader and flatter. The descendants of these dinosaurs were believed to be carnivorous but they have been adapted to eat plant matter too. So later they turned into omnivorous animals.

A report made by the paleontologists proves that the dinosaurs had feathers in their chest, abdomen and back. The large size of these dinosaurs was an added advantage to them as it enabled them of having larger digestive tracts and bigger guts, which helped them in processing the fibrous and tough food of the plant materials, so that nutrients were extracted from it easily.

Some of the feathered dinosaurs like the caudiplex, the beipiaosaurus, the sinornithosaurus, the dilong and the velociraptor are the ancestors of the Tyrannosaurus. Their fossils indicate that these dinosaurs were covered in pro feathers which were simple. These feathers were not designed for the dinosaurs to fly but they helped in the insulation of these animals thus making them very active. These feathers also provided warmth to them. Dinosaurs such as the Oviraptors resembled a lot like the birds of today's time.

The discovery of feathered dinosaur fossils has proved that feathers were a trait of the dinosaur, which was very primitive. The ancestors of both the Ornithischian and Saurischian had feathers too.

# 9. Plant Eating Dinosaurs

There were two food sources that were found on earth for dinosaurs. The primary source was from the plants as the plants were able to synthesize their own foods. The second source was feeding on other animals that where available. This was performed by carnivorous dinosaurs .Herbivorous dinosaurs were well adapted with teethes and long necks to enable them feed on plants. The following are common plant eating dinosaurs in their groups.

## 1. Sauropodomorphs

They are also known as prosauropods. They consist of dinosaurs such as Plateosaurus ,Massopondylus, Lufengosaurus and Anchisaurus. These formed the first herbivore dinosaur to have ever lived on earth. They were able to feed on trees up to a height of 1.2 meters. They had well adapted teeth which were roughened and diamond shaped for easy tearing of vegetation. They had thick muscles at the gizzards that helped in swirling of the food that lead to the foods breakdown. From the gizzards the food was to proceed to the intestines for absorption.

## 2. Ornithischains

They had horny peak that was sharp and protruding out of the mouth for cropping plants. They had different peaks which made them to be divided into different groups where they were to feed on certain plant parts such as fruits for those with short beaks. Teeth were adapted for tearing the picked plant food before swallowing. They had a fleshy cheek covering parts of the side of their mouths. In this group there were dinosaurs such as lesothosaurus, Orodromes and the Scelosaurus.

## 3. Larger ornithopods

They included dinosaurs such as Ouranosaurus, Iguanodonand, Hadrosaurus. They had a beak which was sharp and broad for picking plant foods. They had interlocking teeth for tearing the greens easily.

## 4. Larger ceratopians

They had extremely narrow beak which resembles that of a parrot. The beak was used to feed on vegetation by cutting the vegetation. They had more than one hundred teeth behind the beak; the teeth were interlocking for easy chewing of the plants picked. Example of the dinosaurs in the group includes Psittacosaurus.

# 10. The Weirdest Dinosaurs

For the past couple of decades dinosaurs have been a fascinating species for the humans. With the Jurassic Park series making history on the box office everyone came to have a liking about these gigantic reptiles. Although they perished millions of years ago, still the uncovering of various facts about these exceptional animals is continuing. Contrary to the common belief, not every one of the dinosaurs had streamlined featured as many of them have been discovered to be somewhat weird looking. Let's discuss about a few of the weirdest dinosaurs known to humans.

**Oviraptor-** Looking very similar to modern day ostrich, Oviraptor was weird in the sense that it already had bird like features before it got extinct. Other winged dinosaurs had more bat like wings than bird like as this one did and they incubated their eggs in the nest.

**Ouranosaurs-** They had spines coming out of their backbone which possibly meant either they had sail of frail skin or as speculated by few a hump similar to camel. As it was present in northern African region, hump with fatty tissue can be a possibility and you can imagine how it looked.

**Carnotaurus** - T-Rex, if you remember has tiny arms and Carnotaurus made them look decent enough as it has the puniest ever. And the less told about its weird looks the better as it had horn-like bones coming out of its head and body. It's believed to be a good sprinter with a knack to attack its prey by head butting.

**Suchomimus**- Crocodiles are closer to these dinosaurs than any other. Suchomimus, were actually a hybrid version of dinosaurs and crocs. It lived on prehistoric fishes which it caught using its crocodile like snout although it had the body of carnivore dinos.

**Mamenchisaurus**- Much like other long neck dinosaurs, Mamenchisaurus was herbivore but what made it weird was the length of its neck. An enormous 35-40 feet neck and not surprisingly it could never stretch it to full length upwards. Just imagine how to pump blood 40 feet high!

Hope you enjoyed reading about few of the weirdest dinosaurs ever on the planet.

# 11. The Deadliest Dinosaurs

Just like in today's world where there are deadliest animals in the jungle, during the life of dinosaurs there were dinosaurs that were deadliest. They had features such as dangerous teeth and claws that enabled them be deadliest. The deadliest dinosaurs include the following dinosaurs.

## 1.Tyrannosaurus Rex

It was big in size enabling it be sturdy. It had numerous strong and sharp teeth on its head where it could kill fiercely when circumstances came on its way to kill.

## 2. Utahraptor dinosaur

It had single curved claws which looked like knives. It is believed to have lived over 50 million years ago.

## 3 Jeholopterus

This dinosaur had sharp fangs. It is believed that the Jeholopterus made a living by sucking blood from other dinosaurs such as ponderous sauropods.

## 4. Kronosaurus

This is believed to have been bigger than the present great white shark. It possessed bigger teeth which were scaring. It used to eat almost any creature that lived in the sea. It is sometimes believed to have attacked other land creatures that moved close to the waters where it used to stay.

## 5. Troodon

Troodon was deadly but small, its body weight can be compared to that of a normal human being. It did not possess scaring teeth like other deadly dinosaurs. It was so intelligent that it used to hunt while in packs at night. It had large eyes. When five Troodon came together they managed to be more fierce than a single Rex.

## 6. Allosaurus

This was a fierce predator as it was evidenced by the remains of its jaws which were very strong.

## 7. Sarcosuchus

This can be compared in length to be twice the largest crocodile present on earth today. Its weight can be equal to 10 crocodiles. It had long neck and was powerful to an extent that it can jump out of the water to catch a full sauropod.

## 8. Giganotosaurus

It had a weight of about 8 tones and three strong fingers. It forms the biggest predator ever existed on earth. They were able to bring down a grown up titanosaur .

# 12. Flying Dinosaurs

Dinosaurs were always an interesting species of animals that were around millions of years ago. There were various kinds of dinosaurs in many sizes from large to small. Some were meat eaters while others only ate plants. Most dinosaurs walked the earth, but there were also some flying dinosaurs as well.

*Dimorphodon*

It is a belief that birds have evolved from dinosaurs and although many of these reptiles were not able to fly there were quite a lot of flying

---

dinosaurs during the time these creatures were alive. Here are four of the flying dinosaurs that inhabited the earth millions of years ago.

The **Dimorphodon** is one of the flying dinosaurs that existed during the age of reptiles. This type of dinosaur had two kinds of teeth and it was around 3.3 feet in length with a wing span of 4 feet. Due to its inability to stand and walk, this dinosaur spent a lot of time perched when not flying.

*Rhamphorhynchus*

**Rhamphorhynchus** in another flying dinosaur that had short legs, a long tail that was made of ligaments and its wing span was 3 feet in length. It had a narrow jaw with very sharp teeth and had a beak so to have the ability to catch fish while skimming the waters.

*Quetzalcoatlus*

The **Quetzalcoatlus** existed in North American and is known to be one of the largest flying reptiles during the time dinosaurs were living on earth. Its wing span was 36 feet in length, and it had large eyes, crested head, a very thin beak and its weight was known to be around 300 pounds. The bones and of this flying dinosaur were hallow and due to this and its strong wings it could fly for a very long distances.

The **Pterodactylus** lived nearby water and its diet was of fish and other kinds of small animals. Its wing span was 20 to 30 inches and this reptile had wings that were covered with strong membranes. Due to the way their wings were constructed gave them the ability to fly for a long distance.

# 13. Kinds of Dinosaurs

Dinosaurs were in existence for several million years. These prehistoric creatures were present in different ages such as the Triassic, Jurassic and Cretaceous. Dinosaurs are classified into several types depending on the age they lived, the food they ate or the way they looked. So, what are the different types of dinosaurs? What do they look like? What did they eat? Here is all you needed to know about the kinds of dinosaurs.

Dino Basics

A famous British scientist named Harry Seeley, in 1800's proposed a classification based on their hip structure. Seeley classified two major groups called Ornithischia (bird-hipped) and Saurischia (lizard-hipped). These two types were further broken down into sub groups as follows:

**Ornithischia**

**Thyreophora:** Also known as the armored dinosaurs, these dinos were herbivores (plant eaters) and lived in the early Jurassic to the late Creaceous age. Thyrephora simply means "shield bearers" because these type of dinosaurs had armors, plates and horns. This group included Stegosaurus, Ankylosaurusand Nodosaurids.

*Ornithischia*

**Cerapods:** These are typically horned or duck-billed dinosaurs; this kind had a varied group of dinosaurs like the Ornithopods, Triceratops and Iguanodon. Just like the Thyreophora, Cerapods were herbivores however, these dinos has better teeth that helped them grind plant extracts better and gain more nutrition.

**Saurischia**

**Theropods**: The name means "beast feet" and typically moved on two legs and were carnivores (meat eaters). Some of these kinds of dinosaurs were also omnivores (ate both plants and meat). Theropods lived from the late Triassic period till the end of Creaceous age. Scientist have also found that birds evolved from Theropods. While the scary looking and most popular ones in this category were Tyrannosaurus Rex and Veliociraptor, there were also other dinosaurs like Spinosaurus, Deinonychus, Allosaurus, Carnotaurus, Albertosaurus, Megalosaurus, Yangchuanosaurus and much more.

**Sauropods**: These lizard-footed type of dinosaurs walked on four legs and were enormous in size. They had long necks and tails, were huge in size and had comparatively small heads. Sauropods were herbivores and included Brachiosaurus, Diplodocus, Seismosaurus, Giraffatitan, Apatosaurus, etc.

# 14. The Biggest Dinosaurs

Dinosaurs roamed our earth millions of years ago in the Mesozoic era. Most of them walked on land while some of them had the ability to fly. There were also some who lived in water. The ones that walked on land were known as Archosauria. During the Jurassic period there were many heavy, gigantic dinosaurs that roamed all throughout the earth. Some of the biggest dinosaurs are listed below:

*Liopleurodon*

**Liopleurodon** - Liopleurodon looked similar to an orca and a shark, and it is the biggest pliosaur. It had massive body, huge flippers and a long thick jaw full of teeth. Paleontologists say that this type of dinosaur weighed over 30 tons and could grow to a length of 50 feet.

**Quetzalcoatlus** - This type of dinosaur was also huge in size with its wings spanning to 45 feet. This huge pterosaur has got its name from the winged Aztec God. It led a land bound life despite having the ability to fly.

**Spinosaurus** - Spinosaurus was heavier than Tyrannosaurus Rex hence it is believed that they were bigger in size too. It had a mouth that was similar to crocodile's mouth and it also had a skin flap that protruded from the back which resembled a sail. When their body used to heat up this sail helped to cool down at a faster rate.

*Argentinosaurus*

**Argentinosaurus** - As the name suggests, the fossil of this dinosaur was found in Argentina. It was among the biggest dinosaurs with weight going over 100 tons and height that reached up to 120 feet. One can imagine how big this animal could have been as their single vertebra was around 4 feet in diameter.

**Sauroposeidon** - This type of dinosaur was very much similar to the Argentinosaurus; however, they were about 50 to 60 tons lighter than the former. An interesting feature about this dinosaur is their neck which would grow up to the height of 40 feet.

# 15. The Smallest Dinosaurs

In the Mesozoic Era, 248 million to 65 million years ago, some prehistoric reptiles roamed earth. They greatly varied in length from the largest growing up to be 120 feet long and the smallest one having the same size like a hen. The fossils have greatly helped the paleontologists to discover the smallest dinosaurs that lived on earth. They are as follows:

**The Humming Bird** - It may seem strange but paleontologists believe that dinosaurs did not become extinct completely but they underwent evolution. Humming birds are believed to be the offspring of dinosaurs that lived millions of years ago. It weighs as little as one-tenth of an ounce, and is considered as the smallest dinosaur specie that lives even today.

**Lariosaurus** - With their total weight about 20 pounds and their height from head to tail just about 2 feet, this dinosaur was the smallest aquatic dinosaur. It had a long pointed tail and a streamlined body. It usually lived on water but also lived on land, pretty much like amphibians.

**Pterosaurus** - Pterosaurus had hollow bones and were lightly built. The pterosaurus were of different sizes the smallest one was just a few inches long while they could grow up to 40 feet. They were flying reptiles and had powerful wings that they used for flapping instead of gliding. This carnivore dinosaur ate insects, crabs and fishes.

**Microceratops** - The microceratops were the smallest herbivore dinosaur weighing 4 pounds and their height was just a foot and a half. In order to avoid the onslaught of bigger predators they moved swiftly on their two feet.

**Microaptor** - The microaptors were the smallest carnivore dinosaurs growing to a height of just 2 feet from head to tail. These fascinating creatures could be easily mistaken for a mutated bird. They were also known as four-winged dinosaur as they had feathers on their legs too apart from the arms. Their diet consisted only of insects.

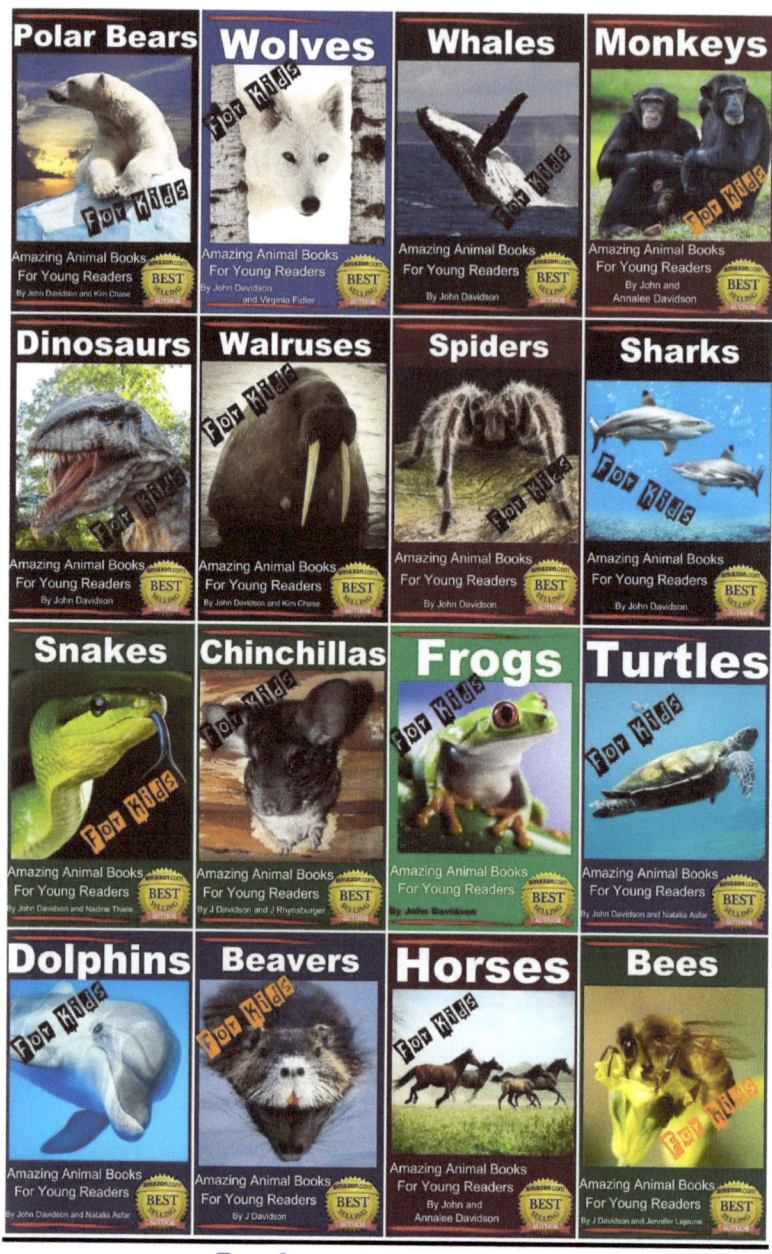

**Purchase at Amazon.com**
**Website** http://AmazingAnimalBooks.com

**Horses** For Kids

Amazing Animal Books
For Young Readers
By John and
Annalee Davidson

**Ponies** For Kids

Amazing Animal Books
For Young Readers
**Rachel Smith**

Ten Amazing Horses For Kids

Nature Books for Kids
JD-Biz Publishing
K. Bennett

Akhal-Teke "The Golden Horse of the desert" For Kids

Nature Books for Kids
JD-Biz Publishing
K. Bennett

Suffolk Punch "The Gentle Giant" For Kids

Nature Books for Kids
JD-Biz Publishing
K. Bennett

Shires "The great Horse" For Kids

Nature Books for Kids
JD-Biz Publishing
K. Bennett

Colonial Spanish "Horse of the Americas" For Kids

Nature Books for Kids
JD-Biz Publishing
K. Bennett

Canadian "The Little Iron Horse" For Kids

Nature Books for Kids
JD-Biz Publishing
K. Bennett

Cleveland Bays "History and Future" Horses For Kids

Nature Books for Kids
JD-Biz Publishing
K. Bennett

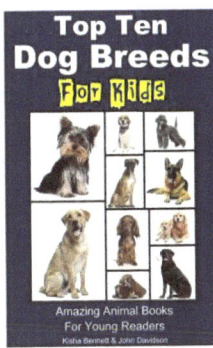

**Top Ten Dog Breeds For Kids**

Amazing Animal Books For Young Readers
Kisha Bennett & John Davidson

**German Shepherds**

Dog Books for Kids
K. Bennett

**Bulldogs**

Dog Books for Kids
K. Bennett

**Dachshund**

Dog Books for Kids
K. Bennett

**Poodles**

Dog Books for Kids
K. Bennett

**Labrador Retrievers**

Dog Books for Kids
K. Bennett

**Rottweilers**

Dog Books for Kids
K. Bennett

**Boxers**

Dog Books for Kids
K. Bennett

**Golden Retrievers**

Dog Books for Kids
K. Bennett

**Puppies**
Dog Books For Kids

AmazingAnimalBooks
By John Davidson

**Beagles**

Dog Books for Kids
K. Bennett

**Yorkshire Terriers**

Dog Books for Kids
K. Bennett

**Dogs**
Top Ten Dog Breeds For Kids

Amazing Animal Books For Young Readers
Zahra Jazeel & John Davidson

**Cats** For Kids

Amazing Animal Books For Young Readers
K. Bennett & John Davidson

**Foxes** For Kids

Amazing Animal Books For Young Readers
Zahra Jazeel & John Davidson

**Wolves** For Kids

Amazing Animal Books For Young Readers
By John Davidson and Virginia Fidler

Our books are available at

1. Amazon.com

2. Barnes and Noble

3. Itunes

4. Kobo

5. Smashwords

6. Google Play Books


## Download Free Books!
## http://MendonCottageBooks.com

# Publisher

JD-Biz Corp

P O Box 374

Mendon, Utah 84325

http://www.jd-biz.com/

Mendon Cottage Books

P O Box 374, Mendon Utah 84325

www.ingramcontent.com/pod-product-compliance
Lightning Source LLC
Chambersburg PA
CBHW050832290526
45792CB00001B/360